The Gunpowder Plot

Helen Cox Cannons

raintree

Raintree is an imprint of Capstone Global Library Limited, a company incorporated in England and Wales having its registered office at 264 Banbury Road, Oxford, OX2 7DY – Registered company number: 6695582

www.raintree.co.uk
myorders@raintree.co.uk

Text © Capstone Global Library Limited 2016
The moral rights of the proprietor have been asserted.

Edited by Clare Lewis
Designed by Steve Mead
Picture research by Kelly Garvin
Production by Helen McCreath
Originated by Capstone Global Library
Printed and bound in China

ISBN 978 1 4747 1435 8 (hardback)
19 18 17 16 15
10 9 8 7 6 5 4 3 2 1

ISBN 978 1 4747 1446 4 (paperback)
20 19 18 17 16
10 9 8 7 6 5 4 3 2 1

British Library Cataloguing in Publication Data
A full catalogue record for this book is available from the British Library.

Acknowledgements
We would like to thank the following for permission to reproduce images: Alamy: Mary Evans Picture Library, 18; Bridgeman Images: Harrogate Museums and Arts, North Yorkshire, Guy Fawkes before King James, 1869-70 (w/c on paper) Gilbert, Sir John (1817-97), 20, Private Collection/The Stapleton Collection/Guy Fawkes, from 'Peeps into the Past', published c.1900 (color litho), Trelleek (fl.c1900), 19; Capstone Press: Peter Bull Art Studio, back cover, 14, 16, 17; Getty Images: Hulton Archive, 4, 8, Hulton Archive/The Print Collector, 13, 15; iStockphoto: Hulton Archive, cover (Thomas Winter); Newscom: Agence Quebec Presse, 6, akg-images, 10, World History Archive, 11; Shutterstock: Beata Becia, 21, Steve Allen, cover (fireworks); The Image Works: Mary Evans Picture Library, 7, 12, Topham/(c)ArenaPal, 5; Wikipedia: Ingrid Brown, 9
Design Elements
Shutterstock: LiliGraphie, Osipovfoto

Contents

Some words are shown in bold, **like this.** You can find out what they mean by looking in the glossary.

What was the Gunpowder Plot?

The Gunpowder Plot happened over 400 years ago. A group of men, including Guy Fawkes, tried to blow up the king and the **Houses of Parliament**. He was stopped just in time.

We remember the **plot** every 5th November.
We light fireworks and bonfires. Sometimes
we put a "Guy" on the bonfire.
This is the true story of the Gunpowder Plot.

How did Elizabeth I treat Catholics?

This is Elizabeth I. She became Queen of England in 1558. At this time, **Protestants** and **Catholics** had been disagreeing with each other for many years.

Elizabeth I passed laws against Catholics. Catholic people had to practise their religion in secret. If Catholic priests were caught **preaching** they were put to death.

Who was Guy Fawkes?

Guy Fawkes was born in York on 13th April 1570. His family were **Protestant**, but his mother's parents were secretly **Catholic**.

This is Guy Fawkes' school as it looks today.

Some of Guy's school friends were also Catholic. Guy became a Catholic while he was still at school. As he got older, Guy became angry about the way Catholics were treated.

War and a new king

Around the year 1593, Guy left England and sailed to Europe. He fought in a war for the **Catholic** Spanish against the **Protestant** Dutch Republic.

Queen Elizabeth I died in 1603. In her
place, James I became king. James's wife
and his mother, Mary Queen of Scots,
were both Catholic.

Did James I improve life for Catholics?

With a new king, **Catholics** in England hoped that things would change. But King James I was a **Protestant**. He passed even more laws against Catholics.

A group of Catholics started to **plot** against the king. They wanted to blow up the king, his wife and their son at the opening of the **Houses of Parliament**. Parliament was where the laws of the country were made.

How did the plotters meet?

While fighting for the Spanish, Guy became a good soldier. He learned to use **gunpowder**. He also met a **Catholic** Englishman called Thomas Wintour.

Thomas Wintour asked Guy to join the **plot** to kill the king. So, in May 1604, Guy returned to London. He met with Robert Catesby, Thomas Wintour and others in an inn. They all promised to keep their plans secret.

How did the plot begin?

By early 1605, there were 13 men involved in the **plot**. They rented a house next to the **Houses of Parliament**. They planned to dig a tunnel from their house to the Parliament **cellars**. But this was taking too long.

The plotters then rented a cellar under the Parliament buildings. Here, they hid 36 barrels of **gunpowder**. It was Guy's job to look after them. He knew how to use gunpowder.

How did Guy Fawkes get caught?

my lord out of the loue i beare ~~vnto~~ to some of youere freud3 i haue acaer of youer preseruacion therfor i would... aduyse yowe as yowe tender youer lyf to deuys~some excuse to shift of youer attendance at this parleament for god and man hathe concurred to punishe the wickednes of this tyme and thinke not saghtlye of this aduertisment but retyere youre self into youre contri whyeare yowe... maye expect the euent in safti for thowghe theare be no apparance of annai stir yet isaye they shall receyue aterrible blowe this parleament and yet they shall not seie who hurts them this councel is not to be contemned becaus it maye do yowe good and can do yowe no harme for the dangere is passed as soonas yowe haue burnt theletter and i hope god will gine yawe the grace to mak good use of it to whose holy proteccion icomend yowe

To the ryght honorable thelord mounteagle

On 26 October 1605, the Catholic Lord Monteagle was given a letter. It warned him not to go to Parliament on 5 November. The letter was probably written by one of the plotters. It was shown to the king.

Early on 5 November, the king ordered his
guards to search Parliament. Guards burst
into the **cellar**. They found Guy Fawkes
with the **gunpowder**. He was just about to
light it!

What happened to the plotters?

Guy Fawkes was taken to the king. At first he would not admit his guilt. But he **confessed** after he was tortured. The plotters were charged with **treason** and hanged.

One year later, on 5 November, people all over the country celebrated the plotters being caught.

Now, both **Catholics** and **Protestants** are free to worship in the United Kingdom. But we still light bonfires and remember what happened all those years ago.

Remember, remember...

You may have heard this rhyme about why we celebrate bonfire night.

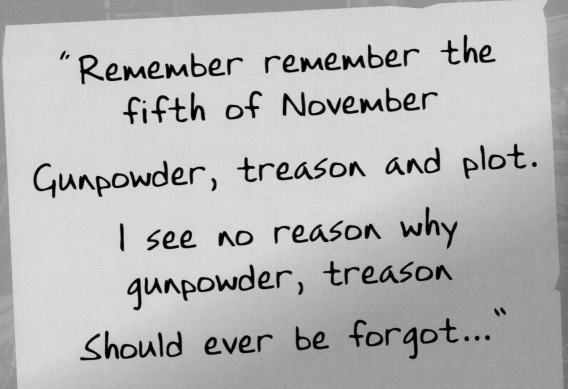

"Remember remember the fifth of November

Gunpowder, treason and plot.

I see no reason why gunpowder, treason

Should ever be forgot..."

Glossary

Catholic Christian who is a member of the Roman Catholic religion

cellar room built underground

confess admit doing something wrong

gunpowder black powder that explodes when touched with fire

Houses of Parliament buildings where the laws of the country are made

plot plan

preach speak and teach about religion

Protestant Christian who is a member of the Protestant religion

treason acting against your country or king or queen

Find out more

The Gunpowder Plot (Great Events),
　Gillian Clements (Franklin Watts, 2014)

Putting on a Play: The Gunpowder Plot,
　Tony and Tom Bradman (Wayland, 2015)

The Gunpowder Plot (History Corner),
　Jenny Powell (Wayland, 2011)

Index